The Empowered Empath

Honing Your Emotional Superpower

Table of Contents

Chapter 1. Introduction

Step foot into a universe of heightened emotion and intense perception in the enlightening Special Report: The Empowered Empath: Honing Your Emotional Superpower. This is no mere report; it's a spiritually transformative journey designed to help you harness, hone, and utilize your empathic abilities for personal growth and the betterment of those around you! Spread across its enriching chapters lies in-depth knowledge about emotional intelligence, empathic abilities, practical techniques to manage emotional energy, and inspiring real-life stories of empowered empaths around the world. By diving into the deep unraveling of this report, you'll find not only learning but also empowerment at your fingertips. This isn't just another product; it's a once-in-a-lifetime opportunity that promises a revolutionary take on your empathic journey, turning the potential overwhelm into your greatest superpower. Magic awaits you between these pages. Come, let us venture together on this mesmerizing journey into the heart of emotional mastery, and emerge as the Empowered Empath you were always meant to be!

Chapter 2. Unveiling Your Intrinsic Empath Traits

Your journey as an empath can be likened to traversing through a vast, luminescent ocean filled with countless emotional energy currents. Each ripple, each wave, each current, carries the potential for transformation. The ocean mirrors the human endeavor for emotional understanding, compassion, and healing, representing the empath's emotional world, with all its unseen depths and fascinating wonders. This ocean, while alluring, can often feel intimidating to navigate without a compass. But fear not, for within you lie the intrinsic empathic traits required to navigate these waters proficiently.

2.1. Understanding Your Sensitivity

The first trait is sensitivity, often considered the cornerstone of an empathic nature. Empaths are naturally sensitive to the emotional energies around them, and often experience them with an intensity unmatched by other individuals. Your ability to absorb and process the feelings of the people and environments around you allows for a level of understanding and compassion that is unique to empaths.

As an empath, you experience sensitivity in layers. The most superficial layer represents the immediate emotional energy from those directly around you; the deeper layers stretch to the extended energies of society, the neighborhood or community, and the universe. Understanding these layers of sensitivity helps you realize the expansive emotional compass that you naturally navigate every day.

Although this sensitivity can be overwhelming at times, remember that it isn't a flaw; rather, it's a unique trait that allows you to connect with the world on a profound level. Embrace this sensitivity and use it as your compass on this empathic journey.

2.2. The Intensity of Empathic Experience

The next trait you possess as an empath is the incredible depth and intensity of your emotional experience. No feeling is merely surface-level for an empath; you have an innate ability to delve deep into these emotional oceans, experiencing feelings in their fullest intensity. This trait can often lead empaths to experience a diverse range of human emotions, spanning from the ecstasies of joy to the depths of despair.

The intensity of your emotional experience isn't just limited to your feelings—it extends to your perceptions and understandings of the world around you. This could be an intense appreciation of the beauty in nature, profound insight into human behavior, or a gut sense about situations and people that often proves accurate.

Acknowledging and understanding the depth of your emotional world is the first step towards empowering your empathic superpower. Use this intensity not to overwhelm you, but to inspire and create a life filled with compassion, depth, and emotional richness.

2.3. Navigating Emotional Transmutation

Empaths have an innate ability to transmute emotional energy—to absorb it, process it, and release it. Just as a prism refracts light into a spectrum of colors, your empathic essence can take the raw emotional energy from your surroundings, thoroughly process it, and release it transformed.

You may relate to scenarios where you've been in a room filled with anxiety and tension, and simply by being there, you've absorbed some of that energy, altering the room's overall emotional climate. In essence, you've transmuted the emotions present. Understanding this ability is key to reclaiming your power as an empath and transforming energy that is not serving you or those around you.

2.4. The Power of Emotional Absorption

The trait of emotional absorption is a double-edged sword. On one hand, this ability allows you to connect deeply with the feelings and emotions of others, and on the other, it can lead to emotional exhaustion if not successfully managed. The key lies in understanding the dynamics of such absorption.

It's essential to distinguish between 'picking up' emotions and 'taking in' emotions. While the former refers to sensing the emotional energy circulating in your surroundings, the latter involves unconsciously absorbing these emotions as if they were your own. Learning to differentiate between the two will help you practice healthier emotional boundaries.

Balancing the empathic trait of emotional absorption relies on two factors: discernment and filters. Discernment pertains to choosing what emotional energies to interact with, and filters refer to the boundary between your energy and the energy of others.

2.5. The Compass of Empathic Intuition

Empaths often possess a robust intuitive sense, enabling them to feel things that might not be evident to the naked eye. Whether it's a gut sense about a person, an insight into a situation, or even a creative solution that appears out of nowhere, your intuition serves as an internal compass guiding you through the complexities of the human emotional landscape.

Learning to trust your intuition can prove transformative, providing you with the resilience to brave the turbulent seas of empathic perception. As you continue to understand and hone these inherent empathic traits and abilities, remember that your journey is as unique as your empathic essence. Embrace your traits, explore your depths, and empower your empathic superpower.

Chapter 3. Recognizing Emotional Energy: An Empath's Atlas

Energy is omnipresent; it isn't limited to the physical realm but also extends into the emotional. Understanding this energy and how it interacts with our own is crucial for we, the empaths.

3.1. The Essence of Emotional Energy

Emotional energy is a type of energy that encompasses the feelings and emotions that every one of us experiences. As an empath, you are especially attuned to this emotional energy. Around people, you've likely observed yourself picking up sensations, moods, or emotions that are not your own. This, in essence, is the experience of emotional energy, something you're acutely perceptive to given your heightened empathic abilities.

3.2. Interpreting Emotional Energy

Just as every person has a unique fingerprint, every emotional energy also carries its individual identity. This identity surfaces through feelings—everything from joy, anger, sadness, to anxiety is unique in its energy signature. Recognizing these subtle differences in energy can be valuable for an empath, allowing you to better understand and navigate the ocean of emotions that you constantly perceive and experience.

3.3. Becoming Attuned to Emotional Energy

Becoming sensitive to emotional energy requires practice and awareness. It's akin to listening to a symphony—you need to identify and appreciate individual instruments to fully appreciate the harmony they create together. As empaths, one way you become attuned to emotional energy is by observing and 'feeling' the world around you, not just with your physical senses, but with your emotional senses as well.

A simple way to practice this involves spending time in silence and solitude. This allows you to observe your own emotional energy, identifying what is truly yours before you start recognizing others'. You could also practice mindfulness wherein you calmly observe each passing emotion without judgment, learning from its nature and its course.

3.4. Emotional Energy and Physical Manifestations

Sometimes, emotional energy can manifest physically. This could be as obvious as a smile on a happy face, or as subtle as a pallor of anxiety and unease. For an empath, these manifestations can act as road signs directing you towards the underlying emotional state.

However, do note that these manifestations are not always accurate representations of the underlying emotions. Learn to trust your intuition as well: your innate ability to 'tap' into the emotional energy of those around you will provide you with additional insight into the true emotional state of a person.

3.5. Acting Upon Recognised Emotional Energy

While it is one thing to recognize emotional energy, what sets empaths apart is the ability to interact with it. You must learn to cleanse yourself of negative emotional energy that you might absorb inadvertently. Techniques such as intentional breathing exercises, grounding techniques, and protective visualizations can help with this.

On the other hand, when you encounter positive emotional energy, you can harness it to uplift not only your own spirits but also those of others around you. All in all, acting upon recognized emotional energy is as much a part of being an empath as recognizing it.

3.6. The Energy of Places and Objects

Believe it or not, places and objects too possess emotional energy. Some places might make you feel comfortable, while others might make you feel unusually anxious or uneasy. This is due to the emotional energy that the place or object holds—emotional residues from past events or from people who've interacted with them.

Learning to recognize these energies can further enhance your empathic abilities. Once you understand and identify these energies, you can better choose the environments that harbor positive emotional energy and avoid those that carry emotional distress.

3.7. Emotional Energy: A Double-edged Sword

It's a wondrous gift to sense and understand emotional energy as you, an empath, can. However, remember that it can also be a double-edged sword. It can bring about deep connections and empathy, but if not managed properly, it can also lead to emotional overwhelm or fatigue.

Practices such as grounding, shielding, and energy cleansing can help mitigate these potential downsides. Remember, as an empath, having self-awareness and understanding your limits is as important as understanding the emotional energy of others.

In summary, emotional energy forms the core of an empath's experiences. Recognizing, interpreting, and effectively managing it can not only help prevent emotional fatigue but also empower your empathic abilities—leading to a more fully realized, vibrant life. This understanding of emotional energy is the core component of the Empowered Empath's journey.

Chapter 4. Differentiating Your Emotions from Others

One of the most challenging tasks an empath faces is the differentiation between their emotions and the emotions of others. As highly-sensitive individuals, empaths absorb the feelings and energies of people around them. This heightened sensitivity can often make it difficult to distinguish between personal feelings and emotions picked on from others. However, with practice and understanding, it's entirely possible to navigate this emotional landscape - to discern your emotions from those of others effectively.

4.1. Why Is It Important To Differentiate Your Emotions?

Understanding your emotions, and differentiating them from those you're picking up from others, is something like cleaning your glasses; everything becomes clear and easier to handle once you've done it. You're better equipped to make decisions that resonate with your well-being, and less likely to feel overwhelmed and exhausted due to confusion and disarray. Being able to identify your feelings and emotions can help develop emotional intelligence, which is a vital tool for managing your mental and emotional health effectively.

4.2. Understanding Emotions as Energy

Emotions are forms of energy that are constantly flowing within and around us. Everything is composed of energy; the universe, the earth, the human body, and the emotions are no different. Each spirit, each emotion, carries with it a unique energy frequency. Thus, this energy can transfer from one person to another, particularly in the case of empaths.

Since empaths are highly attuned to the emotional climate around them, they can often feel and absorb what others are going through. While this makes empaths excellent listeners and counselors, it can also lead to energy drainage, confusion, and emotional exhaustion.

4.3. Techniques for Differentiating Emotions

There are several practices that you can adopt to help differentiate your emotions from others:

-**Grounding**- Grounding is a technique used to regain balance in your life by reconnecting you to the energy of the earth. It allows you to re-establish your roots and steady yourself whenever you feel lost in the sea of emotions.

-**Emotional Labeling**- Start by identifying and labeling your emotions as they occur. Emotional labeling can help create a mental space between you and your feelings, allowing you a chance to examine them objectively.

-**Mindfulness**- Mindfulness practices such as meditation and yoga can create a greater awareness of your inner emotional states and help distinguish between self-emotions and absorbed emotions.

-**Body Awareness**- Our bodies often respond unconsciously to our feelings. Paying attention to these physical changes can give you a clue about what emotion you're experiencing, whether it's your own or someone else's.

4.4. Personal Emotional Check-Ins

One of the most effective techniques to differentiate emotions is to perform regular emotional check-ins with yourself. Below are a few steps you can adopt for the same:

1. Step 1: Identify - Take time to sit quietly and reflect. Try to identify what you are feeling at the moment.

2. Step 2: Acknowledge - Acknowledge the feeling without judgment. All emotions are natural, and acknowledging the emotion can help you accept and process it.

3. Step 3: Question - Ask yourself if this emotion belongs to you or someone else. Remember situations or conversations that could have triggered it.

4. Step 4: Trust - Trust your insights and your ability to differentiate your intuitive feelings from your personal emotions.

This process should be performed regularly, especially when in energetically demanding situations or when you feel overwhelmed.

4.5. The Empath's Journal

Maintaining a daily journal can be a powerful tool for understanding and differentiating your emotions. Write about situations you experienced throughout the day, your emotional reactions, how you felt, and whether those emotions were truly yours or energies you picked up from others.

Over time, patterns may emerge that can further assist you in understanding how your empathic abilities work and when they're most likely to absorb other's emotions.

4.6. Remaining Centered

Keeping yourself emotionally centered is integral to distinguishing your emotions. Being centered refers to staying calm, clear, and grounded in your physical body, regardless of the situations or people around you.

As an empath, your sensitivity to energy can feel overwhelming at times. However, by using these techniques and practices, you'll develop a deeper connection with your emotional self. Remember, the goal is not to stop absorbing emotions; it is to manage and understand them better, therefore transforming this potential obstacle into your superpower.

There's a profound sense of empowerment in understanding and owning your emotions. This journey is an ongoing process of growth, discovery, and transformation - a journey that will change not only how you relate with your personal emotions but also how you navigate the world as an empath. Let your emotional intelligence be your guide, your light amidst the chaos. Own your emotions, and you'll own your power.

Chapter 5. Tools and Techniques for Emotional Balance

Maintaining emotional balance as an empath is as important as the air we breathe. It forms the foundation of our empathic journey, enabling us to fully engage with and navigate the world around us. Achieving emotional balance requires understanding the mind-body connection and employing a range of tools and techniques for self-care and energy management.

5.1. Empathic Grounding Techniques

Grounding, when done correctly, can help you to stay focused and feel safe - keys to emotional balance. Techniques for grounding can range from physically connecting with nature to visualization exercises.

One of the simplest grounding techniques is simply taking off your shoes and planting your bare feet onto the grass, soil, or sand. This process, known as 'Earthing' or 'Grounding,' helps to discharge excess energy and establish a renewed connection with the Earth.

Another effective grounding method is visualizing roots growing from your feet deep into the earth. This roots visualization will help firmly anchor you, preventing the emotional storms of others from sweeping you away. These techniques are best used in combination with deep, mindful breathing.

5.2. Body-Language Awareness

Being an empath means having an innate understanding of the non-verbal cues people unknowingly exhibit. However, being consciously aware of body language can enhance your empathic abilities and assist in achieving emotional balance.

You can understand others' emotions by paying close attention to gestures, postures, facial expressions, and eye movements. Learning to distinguish between your emotions and those you've absorbed from others is a crucial skill that can be improved by sharpening your body-language awareness.

5.3. Emotional Release Exercises

Over time, empaths may accumulate emotional energy that, if not released, can lead to feelings of discomfort or distress. Emotional release exercises can help rid yourself of these lingering emotions.

Methods of emotional release may include journaling about feelings and experiences, practicing the Emotional Freedom Technique (EFT), or using movement based therapies such as dance or yoga. These exercises provide a healthy outlet for emotions, helping to maintain our emotional balance.

5.4. Energy Shield Visualization

An energy shield acts as a buffer between you and external emotional energy. This visualization technique can be particularly effective when in places with large crowds or strong emotional energy.

To create an energy shield, start by closing your eyes, inhaling deeply, and envisioning a protective layer of light surrounding your entire body. This energy shield helps to dull the emotional intensity that empaths often encounter in day-to-day interactions, allowing you to remain more balanced and less affected by others' emotions.

5.5. Practicing Mindfulness Meditation

Mindfulness meditation involves focusing your attention on the present moment without judgment. For empaths, it reinforces the understanding that you are not your emotions. As you practice mindfulness regularly, you become more adept at observing emotions without absorbing them.

There are numerous ways to practice mindfulness, including breath-focused meditation, body scan exercises, and mindful eating. Routine practice can help you develop resilience over time and maintain emotional balance.

5.6. Engaging with Nature

Spending time in nature is incredibly grounding and rejuvenating for empaths. This can be as simple as gardening, walking in a forest, or swimming in a river or ocean. These activities can help you to rebalance your energy and find peace among the natural rhythms of life.

5.7. Managing Emotional Boundaries

As an empath, it's essential that you learn to establish and maintain emotional boundaries. This could involve clearly communicating your needs to others, practicing self-care, and knowing when to walk away from situations or relationships that drain you of energy.

Working on maintaining emotional boundaries can help establish a balanced exchange of energies, protecting you from being overwhelmed by the weight of others' emotions.

Through this combination of grounding techniques, body-language awareness, emotional release exercises, energy shield visualizations, mindful meditation, engagement with nature, and managing boundaries, empaths can learn to achieve and maintain emotional balance. Regular practice of these techniques will ensure that you stay grounded in your empathic journey, truly harnessing your emotional superpower. Empaths are the lantern carriers, the light bearers. While it's a marvel to feel so deeply, it's equally important to keep your own light burning bright, finding your own peace amidst the chaos. Only then can you truly be termed an empowered empath!

Chapter 6. Embracing Your Gift: Self-acceptance as an Empath

The universe spins mysteriously, coursing with a rich tapestry of sensations, emotions, and energies. Vibrations ebb and flow, tugging at the heartstrings of empaths around the globe. More often, empaths, as a result of their heightened sensitivity, experience energy deeply, feeling emotions – both positive and negative — more intensely than their counterparts.

The key to harnessing this heightened emotional superpower lies in self-acceptance, which the following sections explore.

6.1. The Power of Acknowledgment

Firstly, it is crucial to acknowledge and welcome your gift. Listening, attuning, and feeling are natural proclivities for empaths. This intrinsic instinct acts as a guiding beacon, an internal compass navigating through the whirlwind of emotions that swirls around you. Abandon any notion you may hold of your sensitivity as a mark of vulnerability. Instead, understand and accept it as a heightened means of perception, a prodigious power accessible to only a select few.

Empaths can walk into a room and almost immediately perceive the emotional climate. They can tune into a person's emotional state with uncanny precision. They feel the joy, the pain, the love, and the fear that others experience as if it were their own. In other words, empaths have the rare ability to understand the human condition deeply, something which requires acceptance and adulation, not self-doubt or denial.

6.2. The Craft of Understanding Your Emotions

Recognize that as an empath, you have a unique emotional landscape that calls for careful navigation. Being innately sensitive to the emotional energy environment, you need to develop a robust understanding of your own emotions. This is a crucial step toward self-acceptance.

Every emotion you experience is an indicator, signaling underlying needs, desires, or thoughts. Understanding what triggers your emotions, especially the negative ones, can open the door to cultivating positive emotional experiences. Journaling is a potent tool in this regard. Maintain a daily emotions diary, where you detail your emotional experiences and their potential triggers. Over time, you'll be able to discern certain patterns, providing insights into managing your emotional health better.

Remember to be gentle with yourself during this process. Emotional self-awareness isn't accomplished overnight. With patience and persistence, you'll become adept at managing your emotional tides.

6.3. The Art of Setting Healthy Boundaries

One of the pivotal aspects of embracing your empathic abilities is learning to create and reinforce personal boundaries. As an empath, it is easy to get swept away in the tumultuous waves of other people's emotions. By setting clear boundaries, you safeguard your emotional wellbeing.

Arising out of self-respect, these boundaries cater to the realization that your needs, wants, feelings, and comfort are just as valuable as those of others. They serve as your protective shield, aiding you in distinguishing between your emotions and those of others. In real-life situations, these boundaries can translate into saying 'no' when needed, creating space for yourself, and ensuring you're not bearing the emotional burden of those around you unduly.

6.4. The Dance of Self-care

Another facet of self-acceptance as an empath is recognizing the importance of self-care. Emotional self-care allows you to recharge your emotional batteries, preparing you to forge forward with emotional resilience.

Practices such as meditation, grounding exercises, and spending time in nature can work wonders in helping you declutter your emotional space. Engaging in hobbies that spark joy or practicing mindfulness can also add to your emotional well-being. Remember that self-care is not an act of indulgence, but a necessity for an empath.

6.5. The Journey of Self-Love

Self-acceptance is synonymous with self-love. Appreciate yourself for the incredible empath you are! You have the soul of an emotional alchemist, capable of transforming the ordinary into extraordinary through pure understanding and empathy.

Empowering self-talk can fortify your journey towards self-love. Mirror affirmations such as "I am enough," "I am powerful," and "I honor my emotions" can instill a strong sense of self-worth and acceptance. Seeking emotional support when needed, practicing forgiveness, and demonstrating compassion to oneself are other means to cultivate self-love.

In conclusion, self-acceptance is a continual journey for an empath. The power to transform your heightened emotional awareness into invaluable empathy lies in the acceptance of your unique emotional constitution. Embrace your gift with kindness, understanding, and love, for you carry within yourself a superpower that can revolutionize the world around you. It is this deeply intuitive understanding of emotions, this empathetic lens that has the power to foster connections, heal wounds, and create lasting change in the world around you. Embrace it, for this is the gift of the empowered empath.

Chapter 7. Building Healthy Boundaries: Protect Your Emotional Space

As an empath, managing emotional energy is integral to your well-being. The ability to recognize and protect your emotional space is vital in doing this successfully. By building and maintaining healthy boundaries, you ensure that you are not drained or overwhelmed by the absorption of emotions from others. This process takes time, knowledge, and continuous practice. It is essential to approach this without judgement or expectation - remember, having an empathic nature is a unique power, and managing it is a learnable skill.

7.1. Understanding Boundaries

Though boundaries can seem like invisible barriers, they are crucial tools empaths can use to guard against emotional exhaustion. Boundaries, in the simplest terms, are limits or rules that we establish for ourselves to define what is acceptable behavior from others and what isn't. It is a powerful means of emotional self-defense.

Your personal boundaries revolve around your thoughts, emotions, and needs, influencing every interaction you have. Many empaths struggle with boundaries because they naturally feel what others are feeling. Yet, it's crucial to understand that your ability to sense others' emotions doesn't equate to owning or being responsible for them. It's okay, even necessary, to insulate yourself for self-preservation.

7.2. Setting Emotional Boundaries

Embarking on the journey to set emotional boundaries can be

daunting. Many empaths worry about hurting others' feelings. However, setting boundaries is not about causing distress; instead, it's about maintaining respect for your own emotional health.

Start with self-awareness and reflection. Identify situations that often result in you feeling drained or overwhelmed. Note how you respond to these situations. It's during these moments that boundaries may be necessary. Practice mindfulness and monitor your emotional responses. Whenever you're feeling overly drained, remember that it's perfectly okay to say 'no' or ask for space.

7.3. Communicating Your Boundaries

Expressing your boundaries is another step towards emotional self-preservation. Communication need not be confrontational. Here's how you can address it:

- Clearly express your limits. It's okay to say that you need some personal space or alone time to recharge.

- Use I-statements to express your needs without blaming others. For example: "I feel overwhelmed when I spend long hours socializing. I need a quiet break because my ability to empathize can exhaust me."

- Practice regular emotional check-ins with yourself. Are you giving too much to others and neglecting your needs?

Awareness of your emotional state, coupled with clear communication, will help enforce the boundaries you've set. This way, you will not be misunderstood, and others will more likely respect your limits.

7.4. Honoring Other's Boundaries

As an empath, you also need to respect the boundaries of others. Sometimes, your empathy may compel you to overstep, but remember that the key to healthy relationships lies in balance. If someone communicates a boundary, respect it in the same way you would want your boundaries respected.

7.5. Nurturing Your Emotional Space Through Self-Care

Your emotional space is a sacred garden, and it needs regular nurturing. Self-care is an essential part of this process and can take numerous forms.

- Quietude: Regularly spending time alone can help you decompress and separate your emotions from those of others.

- Meditation: It can fortify your inner boundaries and offer a calming space for reflection.

- Engaging in enjoyable activities: Do things that bring joy and relax your mind. This could be a creative activity, spending time in nature, or listening to soothing music.

- Physical care: Regular exercise, a balanced diet, and proper sleep can help the body combat emotional stress effectively.

Developing a self-care routine tailored to your needs can help keep your emotional space healthy, clean, and resilient.

7.6. Overcoming Challenges in Boundary Setting

No journey is without obstacles, and the journey to establishing healthy emotional boundaries is no exception. You may face resistance from others or even question your own decisions. Take heart in knowing that each challenge faced is a step towards honing your skill in boundary setting.

Creating and maintaining your emotional space is a continuous process. It requires patience, resilience, and a powerfully growing understanding of your empathic abilities and emotional needs. There's no one-size-fits-all – your boundaries are as unique as you, crafted by your experiences and needs. With these steps, you're on a path to safeguarding your emotional space, enabling you to harness your empathic abilities healthily and effectively. Remember, setting boundaries is not an act of selfishness but rather an act of self-love. And as you grow and evolve, so should your boundaries.

Remember, the journey is ongoing and ever-evolving. Throughout your journey, there will be moments of success and moments of backsliding. Each step, each misstep is a part of your growth. The key lies in learning from the journey and progressively becoming the Empowered Empath you were always destined to be.

Chapter 8. Harnessing Empathy for Personal Growth

It's often said that being an Empath—having the ability to acutely feel and absorb others' emotions—is a double-edged sword. Indeed, while it allows you to connect deeply with others, it can also lead to emotional overwhelm if not properly harnessed. This chapter is about turning this compelling emotional ability into a definitive power for personal growth.

8.1. Understanding the Empathetic Mind

Empathy is not a monolithic construct; instead, it's a mix of cognitive and emotional components. The ability to put yourself in others' shoes and see the world through their eyes represents cognitive empathy. On the other hand, feeling the emotions of others intensely, sometimes even more than the person feeling them, signifies emotional empathy, often synonymous with being an Empath.

The perspective-taking ability combined with absorbed emotions offers empaths an enriched understanding of human experience. Such insights can lead to a profound sense of self-awareness, thereby fostering personal growth. Moreover, empathy can build resilience, foster creativity, and cultivate leadership, social, and communication skills, all consequently attributing to personal and professional growth.

8.2. Empathy vs. Sympathy: A Clarification

It's vital to differentiate between empathy and sympathy. While sympathy represents feeling 'for' someone—pity or concern—empathy means feeling 'with' someone, sharing their emotional state. This difference is significant for an empath because while sympathy can create a safe distance, empathy often blurs the boundaries, making emotional management crucial for personal growth.

8.3. The Challenging Side of Empathy

It's not always rainbows and butterflies. Empaths often struggle with emotional fatigue, feeling emotionally drained owing to their innate sensibility towards others' feelings. This susceptibility can also lead to empathy-induced stress if not managed well.

Furthermore, empaths can indeed be magnets for emotional vampires—individuals who feed off others' energy. Recognizing such scenarios early on can help avoid significant emotional drainage. Nevertheless, being an Empath, with its accompanying challenges, can also be a journey of deep personal growth and self-discovery.

8.4. Submerged in Emotions: An Empath's Challenge

Navigating through a swell of emotions and differentiating their origin—whether yours or others'—can be challenging for an Empath. This often results in being overwhelmed, creating a sense of losing oneself. A crucial step in personal growth for an Empath is understanding and setting clear emotional boundaries.

8.5. Identifying and Setting Emotional Boundaries

Emotional boundaries serve as your emotional health's protective shield. A practice often neglected in the rush of information and demands of daily living. Yet, it's perhaps the most essential skill to be developed by empaths. Setting boundaries involves recognizing where your emotions end and others' begin—a tricky but rewarding exercise.

Here's a simple technique: Every time you feel an emotional shift after interacting with someone, try to assess—was it your emotional condition before the interaction? A pattern observation can often reveal whose emotions you've been swimming in.

8.6. Techniques to Harness Empathy for Personal Growth

The first step to growth is awareness. Increase attention towards your emotional states; regular self-check-ins can be of help. Develop mindfulness, the art of being present and aware without judgment. Keeping an emotion diary, where you document your emotional journey each day, can provide valuable insights into understanding your empathetic patterns.

Forming connections can lead to transformative experiences for empaths. Networking, mentoring, volunteering—each enables a chance to enhance emotional intelligence and learning about diverse human experiences. Yet, it's vital to adopt a balanced approach—encourage sharing and connection while guarding personal emotional integrity.

Resilience is a necessary element of personal growth for an empath. Simple daily practices like a balanced diet, exercise, deep breathing, and adequate sleep can reduce emotional stress, thereby enhancing resilience.

Finally, remember to take care of yourself—a healthy empath can create healthy relationships. Practice self-love and self-care, as it's equally essential to nurture yourself while you nurture others.

8.7. From Overwhelm to Growth: A Transformational Journey

Being an Empath, emotional overwhelm isn't new. Yet, knowledge, self-awareness, and emotional management can transform this overwhelm into an opportunity—a chance to traverse the deepest corners of human emotions, expediting personal and spiritual growth.

Harnessing empathy for personal growth can indeed be an enlightening experience—the key lies in maintaining balance. A balance between feeling deeply yet protecting one's emotional health—between connecting profoundly with others, yet not losing oneself. Left unharnessed, empathy may lead to quicksand of overwhelming emotions; however, mindfully managed empathy can be a gateway to immense personal growth—turning the empath's story from that of a survivor to a thriver.

In the end, the journey of an Empath is not just about embracing others' emotions—it's about understanding and loving yourself deeper, growing through every experience, and turning heightened empathy into a memorable journey of personal fulfillment and growth.

Chapter 9. The Empath's Self-care Regimen: Ensuring Emotional Health

Surrounded by robust glass walls of perception, you as an empath, tune into the frequency of emotions louder than others. You see, hear and taste feelings that skim by the conscious shores of an ordinary lifestyle, being more susceptive to the subtle nuances of emotional energy around. While this empathic superpower is a gift, a bane lies within its rawness, threatening to toppake the shelter of your emotional health. To ensure you establish strong bounds and maintain your emotional health, we will be discussing the empath's self-care regimen.

9.1. Understanding the Need for Self-Care

The unique sensitivity of empaths allows them to intuitively understand the people and environments around them, often leading to deep connections and profound insights. However, when not managed effectively, these highly attuned perceptual abilities can contribute to overwhelm, exhaustion, and emotional burnout. Enter the necessity of self-care, a regimen designed to guard your emotional health, before addressing the emotional needs of others. Just like the airline safety announcements instruct us to "put your own mask on before helping others", it's paramount to prioritize your wellbeing as an empath.

The value of self-care cannot be overstated. It is not indulgent but rather essential, acting as emotional maintenance that keeps your inner landscape balanced and resilient against the myriad of feelings you absorb daily. Carrying other's emotional weights should come with the reminder to not drown in an ocean of others' emotions. Only by regularly recharging your own emotional reserves can you continue to offer support to others without being energetically depleted.

9.2. The Elements of an Empath's Self-Care Routine

Let us delve into the key elements that form the structural pillars of an empath's self-care regimen. These factors will serve as the foundation for maintaining your emotional health.

1. Meditation: As an empath, your mind is often filled with the feelings and experiences of those around you. Meditation can help relieve the emotional overcrowding. Practice mindfulness meditation, focusing on your breath and the presence of your body, to cast off any emotional residues you have taken on.

2. Boundaries: It's crucial to establish boundaries, both with yourself and with others. The line of emotional separation is often blurry for empaths, leading to unintentional over-sharing of feelings. Learn to recognize and respect the limits of what you can emotionally absorb and handle.

3. Nature: Time in nature can act as a healing balm for empaths. The natural environment provides an open, grounding space that allows the emotions you've absorbed to disperse and neutralize. Make time for nature-based activities such as walking, hiking, or simply watching a sunset or sunrise.

4. Creativity: Allow your empathic abilities to fuel your creativity. It could be anything from writing to painting, dancing, or even cooking. Channeling emotions into creation serves as a healthy emotional outlet.

5. Healthy Lifestyle: Maintaining a balanced diet and regular exercise routine is crucial for an empath's health, as physical

health directly impacts emotional health.

9.3. Practical Techniques for Emotion Management

Empaths often grapple with the task of shielding themselves from an onslaught of emotional energy. Here are some practical techniques that can be integrated into your daily routine to help manage these emotional tidal waves.

1. Grounding Techniques: Grounding exercises like visualizations can help to recast or discharge excess emotional energy. Experiment with different strategies to find what centers you best.

2. Energy Shielding: Visualization of an energy barrier or shield surrounding you can help protect you from absorbing the feelings of others. This technique can be particularly helpful in emotionally charged situations or around energy vampires who drain your emotional resources.

3. Emotional Detox: Regularly detox from heavy emotions by engaging in restorative activities like journaling, baths, and bodywork therapies.

4. Mindful Affirmations: Reinforce your self-care regimen with mindful affirmations that nurture and strengthen your emotional wellbeing such as, "I am safe. I am protected. I am in control of my emotions."

9.4. Empath-Specific Wellness Practices

Beyond general wellness practices, certain strategies specifically address the unique emotional needs of empaths.

1. Solo Time: A significant part of self-care for empaths involves spending time alone. This solitude acts as a buffer, protecting you from the emotional influx of others, allowing you space to process and recover.

2. Emotional Check-ins: Regularly checking in with your feelings can help you discern between your own emotions and those you have absorbed from others. This can be as simple as asking yourself throughout the day, "What am I feeling right now, and why?"

3. Network of Support: It's important that you as an empath have a supportive network of friends or professionals who understand your experiences as an empath. Such communities can provide the space to express feelings and experiences without judgment.

To encapsulate, the journey of an empowered empath is a delicate dance between empathizing with others and preserving one's emotional health. Ensuring regular self-care is vital to an empath's wellbeing. Choose from this myriad of strategies, personalizing them to your lifestyle and preferences. Nurture your emotional superpower by investing in your emotional health. Your journey as an empowered empath awaits a healthy and balanced you.

Chapter 10. Empowered Empaths: Stories to Inspire

A kaleidoscope of stories, of lives lived, transformed, and transcended, awaits you within this realm, illustrating the extraordinary journeys of Empowered Empaths.

10.1. The Awakening: Victoria's Story

Victoria lived her early life with a habitual companion - confusion. As a child, she was continually overwhelmed by strong, all-consuming emotions, which, more often than not, originated from those around her. The intensity was such that she felt like an emotional sponge, soaking up sadness, happiness, anger, despair, from everyone she encountered. The world, in its myriad colours of feelings, felt both beautiful and devastatingly harsh.

It wasn't until Victoria's late teens, when she discovered the term "empath" in a random psychology article, that she had her 'awakening.' She read of individuals who could not only understand others' emotions but truly feel them - just as she did. Simultaneously validated and relieved, she realized she was an empath, undoubtedly. With this revelation, Victoria began her empowering journey, learning about boundaries, energizing and draining entities, and most importantly, harnessing her empathy as a superpower. Today, Victoria works as a therapist, using her empathic abilities to connect with her clients on a profound level.

10.2. Rising Above: Samuel's Journey

Opposite to Victoria, we have Samuel. Born and raised in a family of psychologists, he understood human emotions well. But Samuel was different; he felt them intensely. Despite this, he concealed his empathic superpower, fearing stigma and incomprehension. This led to a turbid adolescence characterized by depression and anxiety.

A chance encounter with an Empowered Empath changed Samuel's life course. Learning from her, he realized that his vulnerabilities were, in truth, his strengths. He started practicing mindfulness, incorporated grounding techniques and built emotional barriers to shield himself from unwanted energy. Today, Samuel advocates for mental health, inspiring countless others like him, proving that no matter how rough the ride, one can always rise above.

10.3. Facing the Storm: Laura's Transformation

Laura, a seasoned nurse, was often commended for her empathy. With time, though, the pain and suffering she absorbed from her patients overwhelmed her. She contemplated leaving her profession, consumed by the emotional fatigue she was facing.

One fateful evening, while attending to a terminally ill patient, she met a visiting speaker - an Empowered Empath. The speaker urged her to see her empathic tendencies not as burdens, but as assets. Referred to a support group for empaths, Laura began learning how to transform her emotional overload into compassion - deep, abiding, and boundlessly healing. By facing the storm head-on, she has not just regained her emotional health but has become an 'Empathy Beacon' within her hospital, guiding others to cope with their empathic tendencies.

10.4. The Altruistic Yeoman: Andrew's Resilience

Born into a family of farmers, the cycle of season-induced difficulties wasn't alien to Andrew. Secretly, Andrew was always in-tune with the communal mood shifts that came with each season. He'd find himself absorbing the collective concern or joy, leaving him emotionally drained and desperate for solitude.

Recognizing his empathic tendencies, he took solace in nature, finding balance amidst the whispering winds and stable mountains. Channeling his empathic abilities, Andrew initiated community gatherings, creating spaces for emotional dialogue and support, transforming his small community forever. His resilience illustrates an empowered empath's potential to become an altruistic yeoman, cultivating not just tangible crops, but seeds of communal empathy and understanding as well.

Each of these narratives reveal empathic experiences varied in their essence but unified in their transformative journey. Your story, yet unwritten, holds the potential to join this constellation of empowered empaths. Let these stories ignite the empowering spark within you, as you move forth, with newfound wisdom and vigour, on your path to becoming the Empowered Empath you were always meant to be. You are, after all, the author of your own empathic journey.

Chapter 11. Channeling Your Empathic Abilities: Future Possibilities

Before we delve into the core aspects of this enlightening chapter, let's acknowledge the beautiful truth that you, as an Empath, are deeply connected to humanity and the universe in ways that many cannot perceive. Empathy is an emotional superpower that allows you to feel and comprehend the emotional experiences of others as if they were your own. And while this emotional affinity can sometimes feel overwhelming, with the right understanding and practices, we can learn to channel our empathic abilities into life-enhancing possibilities.

11.1. Identifying the Potential: The Empathic Spectrum

One of the cornerstones of harnessing your empathic abilities is understanding the empathic spectrum. At one end of this spectrum, we find empathy to be a natural function of human interaction, aiding our understanding and connection with others. At the other end, empathic abilities can be a literal sharing of emotional or physical experiences. Identifying where you fall on this spectrum is paramount to understanding the potential scope of your empathic powers.

Most individuals usually fall in the middle of the empathic spectrum, experiencing empathic responses to varying degrees, from sharing others' emotions to sometimes feeling physical sensations that others are experiencing. Recognizing the extent of your empathic abilities and acknowledging them as a part of your nature lays the foundation for future possibilities.

11.2. Embracing Emotional Intelligence: The Empath's Superpower

Emotional Intelligence is often greatly enhanced in empaths, enabling us to read and navigate emotional landscapes manifested within and around us. It's the ability to perceive, understand, and modify emotions, acting as our guiding compass. This emotional acumen enriches our relationships, careers, and personal growth, facilitating a deep understanding of others' feelings and motivations. By honing this skill, we empower ourselves to become emotional compasses, guiding those around us through shared experiences, understanding, and empathy.

11.3. Harnessing Empathic Energy: Practical Techniques

While the depth and intensity of empathic abilities vary, all empaths can benefit from learning to harness and channel this energy. There are several techniques that can be helpful:

1. Grounding: This practice involves reconnecting with the earth and your own body. It can be as simple as spending time outside, gardening, or engaging in physical activities. Grounding not only aids in relieving anxiety but also enhances your ability to filter energy and safeguard yourself.

2. Shielding: Empaths, given their receptive nature, need shields to protect themselves from overwhelming energies. Imagining yourself surrounded by a protective bubble of light, frequently helps in creating an energy barrier.

3. Energy Releasing: Techniques like meditation, breathwork, or even something as basic as a cool shower can help purge the

body of residual energies collected throughout the day.

4. Intention Setting: Begin every day by setting intentions, affirming your control over your empathic abilities, preventing unwanted energy from seeping into your field.

11.4. Empathic Abilities and Healing

As empaths, our ability to feel deeply and connect with others opens up an incredible potential for healing. While it's essential to draw boundaries to protect our energy, it's equally empowering to use our emotional intelligence to promote healing in ourselves and others. We can aid those grappling with emotions they can't comprehend or handle, as we not only understand emotion at an intellectual level, but we literally feel and experience it. Our poignant connection to emotions is our healing touch.

11.5. Envisioning the Future: The Expansive Empath

Guided by emotional intelligence and investing in nurturing the self, we can envision shaping our future into an expansive landscape. Empathic abilities no longer have to overwhelm us, instead, they should empower us to connect and heal.

We should aspire to tap into the power of this profound connection within ourselves, the people around us, and the universe at large. By honing our empathic abilities and understanding their potential, we can create ripple effects that magnify our personal growth and actively contribute to a more compassionate world.

This profound journey of becoming an Empowered Empath is not just about navigating our emotional world. It involves evolving into healers, guides, and conduits of compassionate energy. In this light, our empathic abilities cease to be just a trait and become a transformative force for ourselves and the world. You have within you the power to change, to grow and to empower - a power that is only likely to grow as you delve deeper into understanding and channeling your empathic abilities.

www.ingramcontent.com/pod-product-compliance
Lightning Source LLC
Chambersburg PA
CBHW070743260726
48660CB00007B/2963